First Edition

Genuine Autographed Collectible

I0063497

Do you want me to sign it in ink or in lipstick?

A Gift of Genius
From The Philosopher Queen

Gift Card

Date:

To:

From:

Message:

What Do Books Do?

BOOKS ARE POWERFUL!

Books **E**ducate!
Books **E**nlighten!
Books **E**mpower!
Books **E**mancipate!
Books **E**ntertain!
Books Spring **E**ternal!
Books Drive **E**xploration!
Books Spark **E**volution!
Books Ignite **Re**volution!

Sharon Esther Lampert

Gift Shop: BooksArePowerful.com

GOD
OF
WHAT?

11 Esoteric Laws of Inextricability

The End of Feel Good Psychobabble that
Numbs the Pain and Keeps Them Sane!
"Only God Knows Best and God Knows Why?"

Self-Help, Philosophy, Spirituality, Religion, Science, Genius, Philosopher Queen Sharon Esther Lampert

GOD OF WHAT? 11 Esoteric Laws of Inextricability

©2022 First Edition by Sharon Esther Lampert. All Rights Reserved.
No part of this book may be used or reproduced in any manner whatsoever without written permission except in the case of brief quotations embodied in critical articles and reviews.

KADIMAH PRESS
Gifts of Genius

Books may be purchased for education, business, or sales promotional use.

ISBN Hardcover: 978-1-885872-005
ISBN Paperback: 978-1-885872-012
ISBN E-Book: 978-1-885872- 029
Library of Congress Catalog Card Number: 2019913395

Author Websites and Emails:
www.PhilosopherQueen.com   FANS@PhilosopherQueen.com
www.SharonEstherLampert.com   FANS@SharonEstherLampert.com

Cover and Interior Book Design: Creative Genius Sharon Esther Lampert

Editor: Dave Segal

Palm Beach Book Publisher, Phone: 917-767-5843, Sharon@PalmBeachBookPublisher.com

To Order Book:
Ingram, 1 Ingram Blvd. La Vergne, TN 37086-3629
Phone: 615-793-5000
Fax orders: 615-287-6990

First Edition

Manufactured in the United States of America

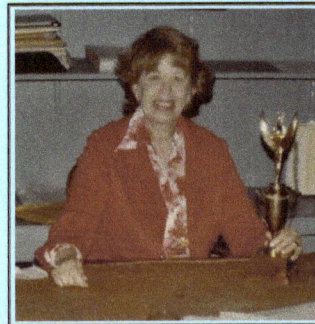

Age 9
THE QUEEN HAS ARRIVED!
My daughter is a poet, a
philosopher and a teacher.
She is the Princess & Pea!
BEAUTY & BRAINS!
LOVE & XOXO
MOMMY

GOD
OF
WHAT?

11 Esoteric Laws of Inextricability

**The End of Feel Good Psychobabble that
Numbs the Pain and Keeps Them Sane!**
"Only God Knows Best and God Knows Why?"

KADIMAH PRESS
Gifts of Genius

BE ART

ART IS SMART
ART IS OF THE HEART
MAKE ART NOT WAR
YOU ARE BORN FOR GREATNESS
YOU ARE A MASTERPIECE

Sharon Esther Lampert

Gift Shop: ArtHeart.store

Dedication

To My Gift The Creative Apparatu

Thank you for the gift of creative genius. It is the seed in me that I was born to be.

MOMMY
LOVE OF MY LIFETIME
WHO KNEW WHO I WAS
FROM THE INSIDE OUT!

Dearest Sharon Esther,

"I want to know God's thoughts — the rest are details."

— Albert Einstein

Dearest Albert,

Who Knew God Was Such a Chatterbox?

GOD IS GO! DO!

God Can Only Do For You
What God Can Do Through You!

I am naked!
I am hungry!
I am thirsty!
I am ignorant!
I have to pee and poop 3X a day!
I am sleepy!

Philosopher Queen, Prophet, Poet, and Prodigy

Sharon Esther Lampert

Who Knew God Was Such a Chatterbox?

And God Said: Go to **Work**!

GOD IS GO! DO!

God Can Only Do for You What God Can Do Through You

God is Not Physics – The Laws of the Universe

God is Metaphysics!

An Invisible and Intangible Entity
Like Your Mind, Thoughts, and Ideas

KADIMAH PRESS: GIFTS OF GENIUS

Read My Books:
"GOD TALKS TO ME: A WORKING DEFINITION OF GOD"
"The 22 Commandments: All You Will Ever Need Know About God"
"Unleash the Creator the God Within: 10 Esoteric Laws of Genius and Creativity"
"God of What? 10 Esoteric Laws of Inextricability"
"Temporary Insanity: We Are Building Our Lives on a Sand Trap" – Written in Letter S

"If I was a Muslim,
they would chop off my head in a heartbeat.
If I was a Christian,
they would banish me to spend an eternity
burning in the inferno of Hell.
But it is the privilege of a Jew to
be able to quarrel with God."

Philosopher **Queen,** Prophet, Poet, and Prodigy
Sharon Esther Lampert

My way toward truth is
to ask the right questions.

Socrates in Plato's "Protagorus"

The hour of departure has arrived and we go our ways.

I to die and you to live.

Which is better?

Only God Knows!

GOD OF WHAT?

What Is God The God Of?

Is Life a Gift or a Punishment?
Measure the Pain!
Measure the Pleasure!

Philosopher **Queen,** **P**rophet, **P**oet, and **P**rodigy

Sharon Esther Lampert

Philosophy is the science
which considers truth.

Aristotle

There Is Only One
TRUTH
No One Has the Truth

Philosopher **Queen,** **P**rophet, **P**oet, and **Pro**digy

Sharon Esther Lampert

All truths are easy to understand
once they are discovered; the point
is to discover them.

Galileo di Vincenzo Bonaiuti de' Galilei

FIGHT TO LIVE
LIVE TO FIGHT
BORN TO DIE

Philosopher Queen, Prophet, Poet, and Prodigy

Sharon Esther Lampert

Beware When the Great God
Lets Loose a Thinker on this Planet.

Ralph Waldo Emerson

THE BLIND LEAD THE BLIND
There Are No Believers
There Are Only Make-Believers and Non -Believers

Philosopher Queen, Prophet, Poet, and Prodigy

Sharon Esther Lampert

We are born to inquire after truth; it belongs to a greater power to possess it. It is not, as Democritus said, hid in the bottom of the deeps, but rather elevated to an infinite height in the divine knowledge.

Michel de Montaigne

You Can Transform Truth into Lies
You Can't Transcend Truth
Transform Information into Knowledge
and Knowledge into Wisdom
There Is Only One Global Enemy: IGNORANCE

Philosopher Queen, Prophet, Poet, and Prodigy
Sharon Esther Lampert

Genius... is the
capacity to see ten things
where the ordinary man sees one.
Poet Ezra Pound

11 Esoteric Laws
of Inextricability

1. **PEACE**LESSNESS
2. **HOME**LESSNESS
3. **LIFE**LESSNESS
4. **HUMAN**BEINGLESSNESS
5. **MORALITY**LESSNESS
6. **CHOICE**LESSNESS
7. **LOVE**LESSNESS
8. **MIND**LESSNESS
9. **HAPPY**LESSNESS
10. **MERCY**LESSNESS
11. **CREATION**LESSNESS

Philosopher **Queen**
Sharon Esther Lampert

Talent hits a target no one else can hit;
Genius hits a target no one else can see.

Arthur Schopenhauer

**Dear God,
Do you even exist?**

**And God Said:
Do you even exist?
Here today – gone tomorrow!**

Philosopher Queen, Prophet, Poet, and Prodigy

Sharon Esther Lampert

Everywhere I go a **Poet** has been there before me.

Sigmund Freud

DEADICATION

Every single second of the day,
A suffering is taking place:
Shake-me. Wake-me. Save me.

Every single second of the day,
My belief in a God is shaken:
Shake-me. Wake-me. Save me.

Death is a greater force than life,
Doctors can't heal death:
Shake-me. Wake-me. Save me.

Evil is a greater force than good;
Judges can't punish evil:
Shake-me. Wake-me. Save me.

Good deeds are fragile glass;
Evil deeds are solid rock:
Shake-me. Wake-me. Save me.

Joy dissipates; Pain endures.
Shake-me. Wake-me. Save me.

GOD IS DEAD.

Poet Sharon Esther Lampert
One of the World's Greatest Poets
POETRY WORLD RECORD "Through The Eyes of Eve"
120 Words of Rhyme from One Family of Rhyme
I Liberated Biblical Eve from 5000 Years of Misogyny

Dearest Sharon Esther,

"Imagination is more important than knowledge. Knowledge is limited. Imagination encircles the world." Logic will get you from A to B. Imagination will take you everywhere. Creativity is seeing what others see, and thinking what no one else has ever thought."

— Albert Einstein

Dearest Albert,

REVELATIONS! **My Books Write Themselves!**

I wake-up in the middle of the night, and write the whole book: Intuition, Insight, and Imagination.

At age 9, my **MOMMY** proclaimed:

THE QUEEN HAS ARRIVED!

My daughter is a poet, philosopher, and teacher!

BEAUTY & BRAINS!

MOMMY

XOXO

No Fakes!
No Fat!
No Fluff!
No Filler!
No Flops!
No F-Bomb!

Sharon Esther Lampert's Mind Conceptualizes

BIG IDEAS

Using One Letter of the Alphabet

What Do Books Do?
—Written in Letter E

7 Goalposts of Education
—Written in Letter E

Sharon's Biography — Written in Letters F, B, and P

CUPID

Language of Love
—Written in Letter C

DESTINY

Are You Living Life By Default or By Design?
—Written in Letter D

Make Life Make Sense

TEMPORARY INSANITY

We Are Building Our Lives on a Sand Trap
—Written in Letter S

PUBLISH: THE SECRET SAUCE OF BOOK SALES
How to Make Money Selling Books
—Written in Letter P

WIN AT THIN

FAT ME SKINNYME
What Works! What Doesn't Work!
—Written in Letter A

Table of Contents

Preface

Disraeli said, "Philosopy becomes poetry and science imagination, in the enthusiasm of genius." This book is a confluence of philosophic genius and poetic genius. It is philosophy condensed into philosophical poetry.

Every noteworthy topic in philosophy is thematically interwoven into a set of unified, seamless, universal, and absolute truths, entitled, **11 Esoteric Laws of Inextricability,** and every single truth, is a timeless truth for all eons.

Finding one philosophical truth is outstanding, but locating, compiling, and explaining 11 philosophical truths is beyond belief.

It has taken generations for a **Philosopher Queen** to be born of this caliber, **who can reduce our reality into single words, that can communicate complex philosophical concepts,** that both students and scholars, will immediately find comprehensible, not to mention endlessly thought provoking: (1) Peacelessness (2) Homelessness (3) Lifelessness (4) Humanbeinglessness (5) Moralitylessness (6) Choicelessness (7)Lovelessness (8) Mindlessness (9) Happylessness (10) Mercylessness (11) Creationlessness. The single thread intertwining these terms, the philosophical concepts, is the poetic genius at work.

Confucius said to his pupil, " Do you think I have come to know many things by studying them? No. I penetrate them by their underlying unity."

Depth Perception: The **Philosopher Queen** in our midst, has revealed to us a perception of reality that is not relative, and that few people have ever laid their eyes, minds, and hearts upon, and has compiled her brilliant vision into one compact book.

Leo Tolstoy said, "There is no genius where there is not simplicity."

In concurrence, **Albert Einstein** said, "When the solution is simple, God is answering." This book will do for philosophy what Einstein did for physics. The **"11 Absolute Truths"** will advance our understanding of our world, and give us a new paradigm of critical knowledge that we can no longer continue to live without. Effulgent, we now see the world we live in from new dimensions. **"11 Absolute Truths"** are culled from an intuitive gift, with no high-tech microscopic or telescopic tools at her disposal.

Throughout history, women have been praised for their deft innate instincts, commonly referred to as, "women's intuition." Finally, we bear witness to the tremendous power unleashed by one woman's intuition that is embodied by this magnificent and monumental achievement.

Robert Graves said, "Intuition is the supra-logic that cuts out all the routine processes of thought and leaps straight from the problem to the answer." This philosophy book is the official vade mecum to attain an astute awareness of reality: **a gem among giants**. – Dr. Chachma

Introduction

God of What?
What Is God The God Of?
Is Life a Gift or a Punishment? Measure the Pain! Measure the Pleasure!
Introducing: 11 Esoteric Laws of Inextricability

For sure, 8-billion people do need the protective services of a supernatural God:

"Please God Help Me, Heal Me, and Protect Me from Harm!"

We were conceived without our consent or consideration. We are forced into being by an act of sexual intercourse.

Upon exiting the cozy womb, and inhaling our first breath, we are immediately scooped up, bathed, weighed, and given a swig of breast milk.

We are completely at the mercy of our parents – not a God.

In childhood, we are introduced to a supernatural God who created the heavens and the earth.

We are taught to worship this God, as a means of extracting from this God the wherewithal of maintaining our sanity, security, and survival.

In every part of the world, 8-billion people pray to a God or Gods, e.g., Muslims pray 5X a day; and Jews pray 3X a day.

Praying to a God for SALVATION is a time-consuming endeavor. Every hour on the hour, our SURVIVAL is in jeopardy: WHY? The 11 Esoteric Laws of Inextricability.

In lieu of a connection with a God or Gods, secular people prefer meditation as the means to foster a connection with oneself for inner well being – to achieve focus clarity, resolve, and resilience before engaging with the demands of the outer world:

We are born hungry and must find a living being/plant to kill and eat.

We are born thirsty and must purify the contaminated water.

We are born naked and must sew our clothes.

We are born in a womb and must build a shelter.

We are born ignorant, unconscious, and irrational, and

must seek knowledge, consciousness, and reason.

How can one ever come to terms with one's life?

Is life a gift or a punishment?

Is one's journey worth the effort required to maintain one's existence?

Wherein lies the secret of the mystery of our existence?

The Bible? The Tanakh? The Talmud? The Zohar? The Dead Sea Scrolls? The Koran? The Gospels? The Apocrypha? The Pseudepigrapha? The Mahabharata? The Book of The Dead? The Granth? The Avesta? The Dhammapada? The Five Classics? The Vedas? The Tao-te-Ching? The Tripitaka?

How interesting is the actual experience of a life?

Here comes the easy part of life: Is waking up each day to go to the bathroom, put makeup up, eat breakfast, go to the bathroom, go to work, eat lunch, go to the bathroom, nosh on a fat-free snack, go back to work, eat dinner, go to the bathroom, remove my makeup, sneak a nosh on a high-caloric snack, get in bed, make love, go to sleep – day in and day out – encircling a twenty-four hour clock, seven days week, 365 days a year, a cause to celebrate or a prison sentence?

On any given day, I am quite dizzy from putting on my lipstick, reapplying my lipstick, and removing my lipstick!

Here comes the hard part of life: The experience of a life is a constant state of war between life and death, between knowledge and ignorance, between health and illness, between sanity and insanity, and between love and hatred. The fight between these opposing dualities is a unrelenting daily struggle. To maintain our survival, our razor sharp swords must always be drawn, and never sleep in their sheaths:

· Farmers fight the noble fight against famine.
· Doctors fight the noble fight against illness.
· Teachers fight the noble fight against ignorance.
· Politicians fight the noble fight against war.
· Theologians fight the noble fight against hatred.

This is why we are all so busy! Each and every day, and each and every hour of the day is a struggle to survive. Every arena of human endeavor is a monumental up-hill climb that requires our unwavering attention. We are all so busy replenishing our daily sustenance: our work translates into money to pay for food, shelter, and cloth-ing. There are a great many more hidden costs involved.

Biological sustenance is a daily struggle and we are all engaged in fighting the noble fight for life itself.

Service to society: Life is interdependent labor-intensive enslavement.

And when we die, we finally have a chance to catch up on our lack of sleep from our exhausting lives — lives that we have had to expend exclusively to maintaining our biological survival.

In the here and now, we are designed not to live forever, but to maintain a tem-porary status, ill fated to weathering the dispassionate storms of life; storms without mercy. Our artificially contrived sense of unfairness, injustice, and inequality take their toll.

Anger looms and lingers right below the surface of most people, from real stresses and imagined slights that we vent upon each other.

And betwixt and between, illness, disease, and premature death follows suit.

Looking forward to our senior citizen years of half-price tickets at movies, museums, theatres, and on buses and subways — that is if you can find someone to go with you who is still alive and well enough to accompany you — is becoming a rarity, as heart attacks and cancer each take their turn devastating our loved ones.

Then there are the genetic predispositions and contagious diseases that threat-en to take hold of us and cause senseless suffering, before those mythological golden years of debilitation and senility set in and ravage us:

" I can't walk well!"
" I can't see well!"
" I can't hear well!"
" I can't remember!"

Oh, the heart wrenching drama of it all!

Inevitably, we have to die and of course, we have to die from something. So be it. Lucky is if you die in your sleep, after having had to take a nap after a tough game of golf, then, you are considered one of the most fortunate ones. Dying, in the midst of doing something you love, dying without having to suffer any more than having had to lose that game of golf is a gift. And if you just have happened to have won that game of golf, what a send off!

Born here, or more matter of factly, forced here without our consent, and operating without a instruction manual, one must join in the daily struggle to maintain one's life, one's family, one's home, one's possessions – only to eventually forfeit it all.

Every material manifestation that we possess lives happily ever after in the home of an heir – or in the local thrift shop.

The futile fight for life ends in naught; they don't even bury you in your own underwear, unless, of course, you plan ahead and write a will, a sign of a truly enlightened being.

Therefore, if given a choice, would anyone want to be born at all?

WHY not let sleeping unborn souls that were resting in peace remain wherever they were and not wake them?

WHAT is it about the experience of a life that is so intriguing that we continue to march on and beat our drums, singing songs of adulation, while weathering the trials and tribulations of our arduous existence?

WHY do we fight the great fight to live here, a place littered with shattering minefields of myriad dimensions of evil incarnate: the daily blood bath of indigenous violence, both intrinsic and extrinsic, between plants, animals and humankind, indigenous natural disasters, and indigenous infinitesimal diseases.

Every single person is living on a private or public battlefield, and has to wrestle with a insane demon of one kind or another: insane work place, illness, insane society, insane environment (nature), insane spouse, insane child, insane parents, and insane self.

An authentic life, where dreams do come true, for most, not for just a minuscule fortunate few; where one's life story is imbued with peace, joy, love, brotherhood, justice, equality, freedom and harmony does not seem possible within these treacherous frontiers.

Few People have Everything.
Many People have Something.
Some People have Nothing.

HOMELESSNESS: Day in and day out, every hour of the day, if you make a wrong move... you will be doomed to death.

For instance, annual earthquakes, hurricanes, and wildfires threaten to annihilate us.

For instance, 24/7 invisible murdering mutating monster microbes threaten to annihilate us. They also infect us and turn us into killers. Vicious viruses infect us and force us to kill our loved ones – not our enemies.

WHY not have this planet that we call "**HOME**," despite the fact, that it will never ever feel like "**HOME SWEET HOME**" for all generations of all eons condemned as too dangerous and uninhabitable?

WELCOME TO PLANET EARTH
WARNING: INSANITY RULES
UNINHABITABLE! CONDEMED!

These are some of the questions to ponder as you read this book. The answers are nowhere to be found, however, after partaking of the philosophical insights unearthed in this philosophical gem, you may mature into a more insightful being than you were before you opened these pages of deft depths. I promise that you will drink from a full cup of enlightenment.

Paradoxically, it is meaningful to write about MEANINGLESSNESS.

Paradoxically, it is divine revelation that inspired this book of GODLESSNESS.

Revelations: My Books Write Themselves! Who Knew God Was Such a Chatterbox!

Sharon Esther Lampert
Philosopher Queen
September 22nd, 1999

Sharon Esther Lampert

11 Esoteric Laws of Inextricability

1. **PEACELESSNESS** Inextricability of 24/7 Life & Death
    - Bloodbath: You are predator and prey. You will kill, ingest, and digest a living being/plant to maintain life.
    - There are 8-million living beings on the planet who fear, hate, and have to eat each other alive to live.
    - A freshly killed carcass/plant will sustain your life — a rotten carcass/plant with kill you with food poisoning.
    - You can kill and eat your own beloved offspring and pets to maintain your life.

2. **LIFELESSNESS** Inextricability of 24/7 Survival & Death
    - You will fight to maintain your life: **FIGHT TO LIVE, LIVE TO FIGHT, BORN TO DIE!**

3. **HOMELESSNESS** Inextricability of 24/7 Security & Insecurity
    - 24/7 The planet is a boobytrapped torture chamber: If you make a wrong move ... you will be doomed to death.

4. **HUMANBEINGLESSNESS** Inextricability of 24/7 Human Animals & Human Beings
    - You are born an ignorant, unconscious, irrational, and destructive human animal.
    - You will be socialized into a human being by a triad of love, learning, and laws.
    - **ALL EVIL IS JUSTIFIED!** 3 GAMES OF LIFE: WIN! WIN or WIN! LOSE or LOSE! LOSE!
    - **DARK AGES:** You talk like a human being, but behave like a human animal.
    - **ENLIGHTENMENT:** You talk like a human being, and behave like a human being.
    - Mother Nature: Poisonous Snakes, Poisonous Plants, and Poisonous Psychopaths.

5. **MORALITYLESSNESS** Inextricability of 24/7 Good & Evil
    - In an immoral world, **GOOD & EVIL** have eight unpredictable outcomes.

6. **CHOICELESSNESS** Inextricability of 24/7 Default & Design
    - 99.9% of people live their lives on a **DEFAULT** setting.
    - Your *DNA* determines the cards you are dealt in life.
    - When you reach age 18, you can start to **DESIGN** your life to fit your personal perogatives.

7. **LOVELESSNESS** Inextricability of Love & Hate
    - 99.9 % of relationships are love-hate relationships
    - 99.9% of people **HELP** you with their strengths and **HURT** you with their weaknesses.
    - For instance: The person you love and married is the same person you hate and divorced.
    - For instance: 99.9% of people do not have to look outside their own families to find hatred.
    - For instance: Most of the hatred in the world is centuries old.
    - You don't find love, you create love.

8. **MINDLESSNESS** Inextricability of 24/7 Unconscious & Conscious
    - You are born ignorant, unconscious, irrational, and destructive.
    - You will attain a small degree of consciousness: educated, conscious, rational, and creative

9. **HAPPYLESSNESS** Inextricability of 24/7 Pain & Pleasure
    - Eating cake gives you pleasure and getting fat from the cake gives you pain.

10. **MERCYLESSNESS** Inextricability of 24/7 Disadvantage & Advantage
    - Your disadvantage is another's advantage.
    - For instance: You arise hungry and at a disadvantage — the restaurant is at an advantage.
    - For instance: You are sick and at a disadvantage — the doctor is at an advantage.

11. **CREATIONLESSNESS** Inextricability of 24/7 Creation & Destruction
    - Creation undergoes Destruction: Decay, Deterioration, and Death.
    - For instance: A ripe lemon offers vitamin C, and the rotten lemon will make you sick, and may kill you.

Philosophical Questions of Inquiry:

1. God of What?

2. What Is God the God Of?

3. Is Life a Gift or a Punishment? Measure the Pain! Measure the Pleasure!

4. Is one's journey worth the effort required to maintain one's existence?

5. Wherein lies the secret of the mystery of our existence?

6. How interesting is the actual experience of a life?

7. Is the 24/7 clock a prison sentence?

8. If given a choice, would anyone want to be born at all?

9. WHY not have this place that we call **"HOME"** condemned as dangerous and uninhabitable?

10. Do our sufferings reflect the natural relationship that exists between all animals, of which we are a full-fledged member in good standing? Is the other not more than mere lunch; the means of acquiring resources that maintain our survival?

11. Do we invent our sufferings and perpetuate them by our ever fermenting irrational hatreds that we then vent upon our own specie?

12. WHY did my cat have to die?

13. WHY do I need a period for 33 years, once a month for a week?

1. PEACELESSNESS

The Esoteric Law of the Inextricability of Life and Death

> With history piling up so fast, almost every day
> is the anniversary of something awful.
> —Joe Brainard

LIFE & **DEATH** are inextricably interwoven into an interdependent matrix. PEACELESSNESS: 24/7 There are 8-million sentient life forms on the planet, and most fear each other, hate each other, and have to eat each other to survive.

Predator & **Prey**: Each of us is both the predator and the prey.

Everyday a bloodbath among living beings is in effect on the land, in the sea, and in the air, in the fight for resources to maintain biological survival.

The violence is indigenous; it knows no mercy, it has no compassion, it has no morality, it is brutal, it is painful, it is treacherous, and there is a continuous and constant suffering. Most predators eat their prey raw – no cooking required!

Canabalism: You and your offspring are edible feasts for the right consumer, or you yourself can eat your own child for dinner to sustain your own life.

LIFE & **DEATH** are inextricably linked. If you want to live, you must consume the life of a simple or complex living being, or ingest a simple or complex living plant. Conversely, You cannot ingest and digest rotten animals or plants. Tragically, if you digest rotten animals or plants, you may die of food poisoning.

ALL EVIL IS JUSTIFIED: Throughout human history, we murder our own species in **WAR GAMES**, but do not feed the human remains to other humans or to other animals. We prefer to let enemy carcasses rot in unmarked mass graves.

During a war, millions of human lives are lost. There is no other sentient life form that murders its own kind in the name of religion or political ideology. Genocide (ethnic cleansing): humans are brutally tortured, and then murdered.

In nature, dead animals do not waste away but are eaten by other animals on land, in the air, or in the sea. An airborn vulture will scoop down for a dead carcass. An alligator will exit the water to walk on land to consume a dead carcass. We murder our own species – but our dead carcasses do not feed the 24/7 hungry. **"Russian Deserter or Russian Fertilizer"** is a popular slogan of the war in Ukraine.

2. LIFELESSNESS

The Esoteric Law of the Inextricability of Survival and Death

"It's only once that you accept that
life is a tragedy that you can start to live."
– Gloria Vanderbilt

SURVIVAL & **DEATH** are inextricably interwoven into an interdependent matrix.

FIGHT TO LIVE, LIVE TO FIGHT, BORN TO DIE!

LIFELSSNESS is a mystery; We are cast into an ongoing movie without a script.
LIFELESSNESS: 24/7 We are forced to fight for our lives every hour of every day, from birth till death. Stop eating and drinking – and you will die.
LIFELESSNESS: 24/7 you life will be extinguished if you don't fight for your life. It seems at first as if you are given a life, however, your life is not your own to do with it what you please. Paradoxically, we are asked to sacrifice our life to maintain our biological survival – and this is the be all and end all of our existence.

24/7 LIFELESSNESS:
1. 24/7 Exertion & Recovery (1/3 of life is spent sleeping)
2. 24/7 Energize (**PEACELESSNESS:** Eat a Living Animal or a Living Plant)
3. 24/7 Defecation: Poop & Pee (3x a day)
4. 24/7 Service to Society

We have to move and not move in accordance with nature. There is a delicate balance taking place between the energy required to move, and then once you have moved, the recovery time that takes place in sleep when you have to stop moving so that you can start moving again.

24/7 We are enslaved in a labor intensive, interdependent network of biological survival. There are 8-billion enslaved workers on the planet (2022).

24/7 Our resources of food, clothing, and shelter have to be replenished, a perpetual state of enslavement. Like squirrels, we have learned how to store our survival food supply for months or years in freezers, storage bins, and basements.

Sharon Esther Lampert

"C'est La Mort"

Of all of our afflictions, the most equally distributed human suffering are the losses brought about by death.

We are all a witness to this very personal darkness, as one by one, every light among us, and everyone we love is taken from us.

We wait and watch, wondering how we will each meet our own devastating doom and final demise.

WHY the commotion when death's grip takes grasp; as if we must have done something wrong to deserve this final decree.

If we are being punished, then it is a collective punishment, leaving no soul among us spared. We are all living our lives on a dead endstreet.

Life is Transient; Death is Permanent.

Too many times, we are done with before we have completed our endeavors, "You have got to be kidding. This is the worst joke I have ever heard."

Death is a humiliating end to a fervent and fanatical struggle to maintain one's life. Especially, after all that time and effort to become a well educated, financially stable, secure, and settled (surrounded by family members); or to finally reach a point when one may have something substantial to offer a family member or the next generation.

Tragically, every generation is left groping around in the vast lightlessness of their existence having to find their way from among the remains of written texts left by the finite few who have been able to create a flickering glint, gleam, or glimmer of light out of the rife darkness.

In each and everyday that lives and dies, the **"Angel of Death"** is always standing beside us, in everything that we do; as death can overtake us at any time during our life: toxic food; treacherous weather; lethal viruses; and fatal accidents in the home, crossing a street, in a car, plane or drowning in the water.

CURVE BALLS: Without warning, on land, sea or air, danger hovers and one's life can be revoked instantaneously.

As I was editing this book, the world reknown vocalist Celine Dion was inflicted with a cruel rare medical disorder, **Stiff Person Syndrome**, at the young age of 54.

Recently, my dear fried Lenny Guttman was hospitalized with an emergency **Septic Shock Infection** that left him unable to move his limbs. Thanks to antibiotics, he is recovering. Last week, he was walking with the help of a walker. He survived.

Inevitably and eventually, each and every life is snuffed out or snuffs itself out like a flickering melting candle. The "Angel of Death" is the final victor.

Light is Momentary; Darkness Prevails.

In our finite days, with every turn of the earth's axis, we sneak a peek at the new generation of people who may inhabit our homes and must water our lawns.

Well, however our individual cards play out, we did not exist for most of the history of the world and we will not exist for most of the world's inevitable future.

Life is Short; Death is Long.

"C'est La Vie"

In summation, all the **absolute truths**, compiled and presented here for the very first time, ever in the history of our civilization, are aesthetically indigestible, however, they may prove to be the antidote to unveiling a greater connection to ourselves, in body, spirit, and mind.

Most certainly, we will develop a deepening, awakening consciousness that can enter the hearts of the living and propel civilization forward in search of a possible shared humanity of respect, compassion, and peacefulness.

Possible, however, not probable; the meaning of LIFELESSNESS is incomprehensible.

Life is Finite; Death is Final.

3. HOMELESSNESS

The Esoteric Law of the Inextricability of Security and Insecurity

WELCOME TO PLANET EARTH
INSANITY RULES
CONDEMNED. UNINHABITABLE.

Philosopher Queen Sharon Esther Lampert

SECURITY & **INSECURITY** are inextricably interwoven into an interdependent matrix. HOMELESSNESS: Planet Earth is a booby-trapped torture chamber. Danger manifests everywhere, and is innately inherent in every experience and endeavor.

HOMELESSNESS: If you make a wrong move, you will be doomed to death:
If you eat food, you may develop food poisoning.
If you swim in the ocean, you may drown.
If you sit the hot sun, you may burn.
If you sit in the cold, you may freeze.
If you cross a street, you may get hit by a speeding car.
If you fly on an airplane, it may crash.
If you drive a car, you may have a fatal accident.
If you make love to the wrong person, you may die from AIDs.
If you are allergic to strawberries and eat one, you may die in an instant!
If you encounter a wild animal... you will be killed and eaten for lunch.
If you encounter a human animal.. you will be murdered, and left to rot.
If you are infected by an invisible-murdering-mutating microbe, you may die and you will in turn infect and murder your loved ones — not your enemies.

HOMELESSNESS: Nature's wrath is a daily occurrence that devastates and destroys lives in a matter of minutes: earthquakes, hurricanes, tornadoes, floods, blizzards, avalanches, wildfires, erupting volcanoes, and heat waves.
HOMELESSNESS: Unmitigated suffering from genetic diseases, and contagious diseases wipe out millions of people in a heartbeat: AIDS.
24/7 We will never be able to feel HOME-SWEET-HOME on this planet: yesterday, today, tomorrow, and forevermore!

4. HUMANBEINGLESSNESS

The Esoteric Law of the Inextricability of the Human Animal and Human Being

Dark Ages:
When You Talk Like a Human Being and
Behave Like a Human Animal

Enlightenment:
When You Talk Like a Human Being and
Behave Like a Human Being

Sharon Esther Lampert
Philosopher Queen

The **Human Animal** and the **Human Being** are inextricably interwoven into an interdependent matrix.

NATURE:HUMAN ANIMAL
NURTURE: HUMAN BEING

WILD ANIMALS ARE DOMESTICATED   HUMAN ANIMALS ARE SOCIALIZED

The human being is an "**artificial construction,**" socialized to live in a civilization by the triad of love, learning, and laws.

THE BLIND LEAD THE BLIND
ALL EVIL IS JUSTIFIED!
EVIL: THE DOUBLE WHAMMY OF
NASTY NATURE & NASTY NURTURE

Human Animals Are Socialized and Schizophrenic

When you see a person behaving well, with social graces and manners, that person has been socialized, and is exhibiting artificially-contrived behaviors.

Every person has to navigate the difficult emotional terrain between the natural and innate animal instinct, and the artificially-contrived social behaviors set forth by the civilized society in which they live — and a schizophrenia sets in.

In the the public domain, people learn to behave with manners and social graces, and in the private domain, people continue to exhibit their natural and innate animal instincts.

Bar-Mitzvah Blues

During college, my part-time job was teaching children and adults to read Hebrew in preparation for their Bar & Bat-Mitzvahs (a photograph of me and my class was published in the book, "Jewish & Female by Susan Weidman Schneider, 1984).

There is usually a 15-minute break for snacks, for cookies and juice. When the cookies are displayed on the table, one child, a boy, quickly runs to the plate of cookies, and fills his pocket with ten cookies, not thinking about whether there will be enough cookies for the other children.

When I approach him and explain the situation, that there are not enough cookies for the other children and, it is important to learn how to share, he asks me these questions:

"What could possibly be good about sharing?'

"I now have ten cookies, and if I share, I will only have two cookies."

"Why is sharing good?"

"Why should I learn to share?"

As a Hebrew school teacher, I am supposed to have the right answer to these ethical questions, however, I am much more than a normal Hebrew-school teacher, I am also a **Philosopher** Queen; and I know that he is a human animal, and as a human animal, he is doing a great job and I should applaud him with accolades:

1. He sees the cookies.

2. He runs fast.

3. He stuffs his pockets with ten cookies.

4. He has cookies for today and perhaps tomorrow.

5. He can trade extra cookies for services from friends.

He is following his natural and innate animal instincts of survival. I should applaud him, however, my job is to castigate him, and transform him into someone he is not – a human being.

I am asking him to learn to behave in a way which is contrary to his natural and innate animal instincts – and a schizophrenia develops in him; the schizophrenia between his natural and innate animal instinct, and his learned socialized behaviors that are required of him to live in a civilization.

He has to learn to live in an artificially-contrived environment that is often contrary to his natural animal instincts. This is precisely where his emotional problems begin and end, and for that matter, this is also the crux of the matter, for most of the other emotional problems of every person who is living within a society.

It is difficult to maintain the delicate balance because from the personal to the private, because you have two personas that are in opposition to each other.

For instance, in a civilized Hebrew-school society, the artificially-contrieved rule is that every child will get one cookie, and if there are enough cookies for all of the children, then each child will get two cookies, or if there are only five cookies left on the plate, I may raffle them off to the child who knows the answer to a Jewish-trivia question.

African Farmers vs. Elephants

Nature, a weekly television show on channel 13, had a program on the wild elephants in Africa. The elephants would venture into the fields of the farmers, and eat their crops during the night. Farmers would kill the invading elephants. LOSE! LOSE! GAMEPLAN

The only way to stop the elephants was to capture them, domesticate them, and use them for transportation.

The farmers would then be in charge of feeding them, and the elephants no longer ravaged the farmers crops.

People and elephants were working in unison, exchanging needs in order to survive and coexist. In sum: Socialization of human animals and domestication of wild animals working in unison is a WIN! WIN! GAMEPLAN (collaboration)

5. MORALITYLESSNESS
The Esoteric Law of the Inextricability of Good and Evil

"You Can Do It All Right and Get It All Wrong, or
You Can Do It All Wrong, and Get It All Right"
Sharon Esther Lampert
Philosopher Queen

Can you lead a moral life in an immoral world?

GOOD & EVIL are inextricably interwoven into an interdependent matrix.
MORALITYLESSNESS: In an immoral world, GOOD & EVIL have eight unpredictable outcomes:
1. Good can lead to a greater good
2. Good can lead to good & evil
3. Good can lead to evil
4. Evil can lead to a greater evil
5. Evil lead to good & evil
6. Evil lead to a greater good
7. Good can lead to nothing.
8. Evil can lead to nothing.

For Instance:
MALALA: Evil Leads to a Greater Good
When Malala was shot in the head by a Taliban terrorist in Pakistan, she was airlifted to the United Kingdom, and reaped many rewards and awards:
· She earned a fi rst-rate education in the United Kingdom.
· She was honored with a Nobel Prize.
· She raises money to educate women in third-world countries.

For Instance:
MARTHA SMART: Good Leads to Evil and Evil Leads to a Greater Good
Martha Smart's father gave a homeless man a job, and the man abducted his 14-year old daughter, and drugged and raped her every day for nine months.
· Martha Smart is an international advocate on behalf of abducted children.

6. CHOICELESSNESS
The Esoteric Law of the Inextricability of Default and Design

Living your life by **DEFAULT** and **DESIGN** are inextricably interwoven into an interdependent matrix. You have to play the cards you are dealt in life – what you do with the cards you are dealt in life determines your destiny.

CHOICELESSNESS: You have no say over the most important decisions in your life. Vital decisions are made for you without your consent or consideration:

1. When you are born and when and how and when you will die
2. Your DNA: Height, Eye Color, Body Type, Gifts and Talents
3. Your Parents
4. Your Religion
5. Your Nationality
6. The Language You Speak
7. Your Early Education and Social Conditioning
8. Your Allies & Enemies
9. Life's Vicissitudes

DEFAULT: Ages: Birth –18

99.9% of people live their lives by **DEFAULT**. We are born into authoritarian birth bubbles. Our parents dictate our lives and are our first role models. On one hand, your **DEFAULT** setting may have been a blessing – and not a curse. On the other hand, if your disagree with your programming, it may be construed as a rebellious act. Your personal affinities will be dismissed if they conflict with the norms of your culture. Any deviation from the norms of your culture will be frowned upon, and you may even be excommunicated and abandoned like a stray dog on the street.

DESIGN: Ages 18+

Once you reach the legal age of 18, you can set yourself free from your **DEFAULT** setting, and begin the journey of making choices that take into account your personal preferences and perogatives. You will always bear the imprint of your **DEFAULT** setting, even as you make course corrections and live your life by **DESIGN**.

7. LOVELESSNESS
The Esoteric Law of the Inextricability of Love and Hate

LOVE & **HATE** are inextricably interwoven into an interdependent matrix.

LOVELESSNESS
All people **HELP** you with their strengths and **HURT** you with their weaknesses!

99.9% of personal & professional relationships are **Love & Hate** relationships.

99.9% of people do not have to look outside their own families to find hatred.

99.9% of relationships are infected with: "Dysfunctional Domestic Drama"

Conditional love: People don't love you, they love only want they want from you!

Most people do not have enough love to love themselves — let alone to love you!

99.9% of the hatred in the world is centuries old!

99.9% of people have to learn how to love themselves

Premise 1. You Can Never Know Another Person
· The person you love and married is the same person you hate and divorced.
· You marry a stranger.
· You have sex with a stranger.
· You have children with a stranger.
· You divorce a stranger.
· 50% of couples are trying to get into a relationship — while the other 50% of couples are trying to get out of a relationship.

Premise 2. You Don't Find Love, You Create Love: Respect, Kindness, Understanding Empathy, and Compassion
1. True love is real, but rare.
2. True love is unconditional love
3. The loss of true love is excruciating, and time cannot not heal the heartbreak.

Premise 3. The Most Important Relationship is the One You Have with Yourself
1. Self-love is true love. Love from outside of yourself is **BONUS LOVE**.

8. MINDLESSNESS
The Esoteric Law of the Inextricability of Unconscious and Conscious

UNCONSCIOUS and **CONSCIOUS** are inextricably interwoven into an interdependent matrix. We are born into the world unconscious, irrational, ignorant, and destructive.

MINDLESSNESS: The state of consciousness is not possible – only an approximation or a matter of degree of consciousness is attainable.

We have faulty memories and must learn and relearn whatever we are taught, time and again. In old age, debilitation, senility, and dementia robs us of our minds.

Education, therapy, and meditation are some of the means available to achieve a degree of consciousness, and these modalities have inherent limitations.

We live in a triple fog: mind fog, body fog, and world fog:

Mind Fog:
The first fog is the fog that exists inside of our own minds. Our ideas, thoughts, and feelings are invisible and intangible entities. We fear LIFE! We fear DEATH!

Body Fog:
The second fog is the fog that exists inside of our bodies. People live inside of bodies that they do not understand. Our bodies are on autopilot. We do not turn our bodies on or turn them off. We must eat and drink 3X a day to keep our bodies turned on.

World Fog:
The third fog is that we don't understand the world that exists around us. 8-million sentient life forms inhabit our world – most are living their lives on autopilot.

We know that we were not in existence for most of the history of the world, and we will not be in existence for most of the future of the world beyond our finite lifespans. Life has no rhyme, reason, or meaning, however, we instinctively cling to life, and fight for life – until death do us part.

The WHY? of Existence : The Ever Impenetrable Fourth Fog

It is hard for me to fathom the fact that billions of people lived and died on Planet Earth, before the day I arrived, and that the world is still engaged in bloody-battlefield wars and genocide that span weeks, months, and years. People across the globe experience famine, poverty, and suffer the indignity of ignorance due to the lack of an education.

The world we inhabit operates according to dynamics that are beyond our understanding, and beyond our control.

We don't flip a switch and turn the sun, moon or stars on or off.

Our lives are a precarious happening in history. We don't ask to be born, however, we are forced here, and thrust into circumstances that are not of our choice.

Most of our lives will come and go very quickly, and are of no earth shattering consequence.

Most of us will soon be forgotten by our closest loved ones, until of course, reflective glimpses of our physical or spiritual selves appear within their reflective mirrors.

We will live longer life spans than our cherished pets, but shorter life spans than many species of trees.

In light of what we are able to comprehend, artificial fictions abound in every facet of our lives.

Each person is besieged with having to qualify every statement that is heard with, "Is it true?" or "Is it false?"

Our minds ask these questions all day, and everyday, with the hope of attaining a discernible glimmer of a comprehensible picture of an objective truth that exists outside of our subjective minds.

We are unceasingly engaged with making sense out of our perplexing, puzzling, and paradoxical existence.

How many people know their own minds, or understand how the bodies that they occupy function, or comprehend the world around them – even though we have an intimate experience of our own minds, inhabit our own bodies, and interact with the world, day in and day out.

Perhaps, it is explainable by the understanding that we have had to ingest, digest, and absorb many artificial fictions about ourselves, and about our existence;

and this blinding fogginess, a white fog, leaves each and every generation, living in a state of chaos, conflict, and confusion.

We forge ahead, with invention and innovation in science, medicine, computers, technology and space travel; but more often, we rage ahead, with daily civil and international strife.

When our barbarous temper boils over, we embroil ourselves in blood-curdling genocide. Acts of genocide cross all civilizations and all continents: Armenians, European Jews, Cambodians, Native Americans, Nanking Massacres of the Chinese, Tibetans, Rwandans, Bosnians, Kosovo Albanians, and East Timorians.

A case can be made, that we lack a capacity to decipher the true state of our existence – and make light of it. As a result, our artificial fictions make the most sense that is possible, in a given time and place in history.

The choices we made were based on the artificial fictions we believed in at that time. We pay a steep price as we become part of the imperfect problem, instead of becoming part of the imperfect solution. We have had no other choice, as we were unable to choose, having ingested and digested so many artificial fictions that were poisonous to our mind, heart, and soul.

Our decisions were colored by extreme emotional states, blinding rages of pure hatred for ourselves, and of the other.

We are figuratively and literally willing to pay an arm and a leg as well as give an arm and a leg for more guns, more bombs, more hand grenades and more land mines.

If we had to grade ourselves, our report card would read, an A in effort in manufacturing weapons of mass destruction: nuclear, biological, and chemical warfare, and a D in self-love, and an F in self-control.

The other they must die for one reason or another, and we are willing to sacrifice ourselves to get the job done.

In lieu of what we have been able to accomplish to dignify our lives through science, medicine, and technology, we continue to cheapen our lives through the desecration of war and genocide.

The devastation of ourselves and of the other makes the most sense.

Simply, MIGHT = RIGHT. All other resolutions become unintelligible.

In a war, we are willing to have ourselves killed to defend our artificial fictions. The killing of millions is acceptable in a state of war.

When we go to war, however, death and destruction of thousands becomes our only resolve. WAR is a LOSE! LOSE Gameplan. The objective is to put the other in the cemetery. Billions of dollars of resources are squandered. **ALL EVIL IS JUSTIFIED!**

It is time to make international laws that state that war is illegal, and that governments must do everything in their power to prevent them.

Our soldiers should be put out to pasture, and reassigned to life-sustaining objectives.

How is it that we forget that it is our beloved children that we send to fight our wars for us.

What gives us the right to sacrifice our beloved children in the prime of their lives to solve problems? This is institutionalized child abuse.

Every nation across the globe creates an indestructible army of destructible soldiers. Both sides of a battlefield will be dismembered limb by limb, before all limbs become completely severed, only then, will it be deemed a completely reasonable and rational choice to surrender with the one remaining limb, and raise a white flag.

What in the whole wide world could possibly be worth all that effort? And if a country can strive to produce such a seemingly effortless task of destruction, why can't the same massive effort be used to promote life?

After the gut-wrenching drama of war unfolds, the soldiers who survive are plagued by incurable traumas.

Our victorious soldiers return home and become our broken children.

Many future generations are damaged from the effects of war on previous generations.

After the dead have been buried, we will all agree that war is the wrong choice, that tomorrow is a new day and change is possible, and that this was the last war, however, in each and every generation, the infernos of hatred are inextinguishable, and the resulting bonfires of war engulf us once again.

War is a billion dollar profitable enterprise; education is a non-profit enterprise.

Our artificial fictions manifest themselves everywhere, at any given time and place.

Moreover, most of our own personal lifetime experiences fade fast into oblivion. Our human memory is a subjective experience that is faulty and fleeting.

Our only recourse is the written word. The written word helps us keep track of where we have been, where we are, and where we are going; and is our only means of remembering the **WHAT? WHO? WHEN?** and **WHERE?** of our experience. The WHY? of our existence is the ever impenetrable fourth fog.

9. HAPPYLESSNESS
The Esoteric Law of the Inextricability of Pleasure and Pain

In her diary, just days before her death,
Frieda Kahlo penned her final entry stating:
I hope the exit is joyful - and I hope never to return."
– Frieda Kahlo

PLEASURE & PAIN are inextricably interwoven into an interdependent matrix. HAPPYLESSNESS: Cake brings us pleasure & getting fat from cake brings us pain.

HAPPYLESSNESS: For instance, one of the greatest joys of life is the blessing of giving birth to a healthy baby – even if the birth of the baby entails excruciating pain to the mother.

HAPPYLESSNESS AND LIFELESSNESS: For instance, we comfort a crying baby who is in distress because of hunger and a wet diaper. First day of life: the pain of hunger, and the pleasure of breast milk, and the fight for survival.

HAPPYLESSNESS: For instance, as the crawling baby metamorphosed into a walking toddler, the **pain** & **pleasure** of falling and walking sets the stage for the continuous undulating state of the **pain** & **pleasure** of failing and succeeding that is inextricably integral to the undulating peaks & pits of life's daily vicissitudes.

HAPPYLESSNESS AND PEACELESSNESS: For instance, you will inflict pain on a living animal to kill it to eat it – and simultaneously, the ingestion of the animal will bring you pleasure. HAPPYLESSNESS: One animal's pain is another animal's pleasure.

HAPPYLESSNESS IN SPORTS: For instance, every sport played has a winner and a loser. At the final buzzer, the winning team is celebrating with a bottle of champange, while the losing team is devastated, depressed, and dejected.

HAPPYLESSNESS: ANOTHER SCHOOL SHOOTING MASSACRE
For instance, in the school shooting in Parkland Florida, 17 students were brutally murdered, and 17 other students were brutally shot and will have to live out their lives with bullet fragments lodged deep inside of their bodies. They simultaneously feel the pleasure of survival & the pain of their indelible wounds.

10. MERCYLESSNESS

The Esoteric Law of the Inextricability of Advantage and Disadvantage

MERCYLESSNESS: ADVANTAGE and **DISADVANTAGE** are inextricably interwoven into an interdependent matrix.

> "A Jewish woman had two chickens.
> One got sick, so the woman made chicken soup
> out of the other one to help the sick one get well.
> Henny Youngman

MERCYLESSNESS: For every disadvantage, there is someone who will gain an advantage and benefit from your disadvantage. You are either on the side of **ADVANTAGE** or you on the side of **DISADVANTAGE**:

HUNGER: For instance, you are hungry, and want to eat something. You are hungry, so you are on the side of the disadvantage. You have many choices: You can grow the food, you can purchase the food in a supermarket, or you can make a restaurant reservation! The supermarket or restaurant are on the side of the advantage. We are usually hungry at least three times a day, a recurrent state of perpetual disadvantage. We ake up hungry and disadvantaged.

ILLNESS: For instance, you don't feel well. You call a doctor and make an appointment. You are ill and on the side of the disadvantage, and the doctor is on the side of the advantage.

IGNORANCE: For instance, you are ignorant and have to get an education. You are on the side of the disadvantage, and the teacher and school are on the side of the advantage.

SEXISM: For instance, you are born female, and the male gender disinfranchises you as being of lesser value than being born an advantageous male.

RACISM: For instance, you are the minority – and the majority disinfranchises you as being of lesser value than the advantageous majority.

SPORTS: For instance, in football, you foul a player on the opposing team, and the opposing team is awarded a penalty kick, scores a goal, and wins the game. Your disadvantage is their advantage and ultimately their victory.

11. CREATIONLESSNESS
The Esoteric Law of the Inextricability of Creation and Destruction

CREATION and DESTRUCTION are inextricably interwoven into an interdependent matrix.

CREATIONLESSNESS: Everything we create will undergo: decay, decomposition, downgrade, decline, destruction, deterioration, disease, and death.

CREATIONLESSNESS: We have to replenish all of our resources. Our food supply undergoes decay, our clothes undergo deterioration, our car is downgraded the day after we purchase it. Our computers have a 3-year shelf life.

CREATIONLESSNESS: We create life by sexual intercourse – even though we know that all life created will be doomed to disease and death.

CREATIONLESSNESS: For instance, you plant a lemon tree, and gather your ripe lemons. Lemons are nutritious and packed with vitamin C. Lemons can be stored at room tempreture for a week, or stored in the refrigerator for a 4-6 weeks, or stored in the freezer for 3-4 months. The same lemon that boosted your intake of vitamin C, and helped you ward off the common cold – is the same expired lemon that will undergo decay and decomposition, and will may make you sick from food poisoning, and may even kill you.

CREATIONLESSNESS: For instance, when your immune system is robust, you are healthy and your body is able to fight off invaders: bacteria, viruses, and toxins. When your immune system is weak, you will catch a cold, a flu, or a virus. As you age, your health will decline, and your immune system's efficiency will decrease and be downgraded – until the finality of disease, senility, and death.

CREATIONLESSNESS: In wars, we willfully drop billion-dollar bombs to destroy our enemies. In minutes, thousands of years of a civilization is destroyed. We turn our own children into soldiers who kill and will be killed.

CREATIONLESSNESS: We are born ignorant, irrational, unconscious, and destructive. Any toddler can throw a drinking glass on the floor, and smash it into smithereens of shards of glass that cannot be glued back together. Death is a greater force than life. Life is finite; death is final.

Dr. Admiral Leonard H. McCoy "Bones"
USS Enterprise
23rd & 24th Centuries

McCoy:
"We were speculating. Is God really out there?"

Captain James T. Kirk
USS Enterprise
23rd & 24th Centuries

Kirk:
"Maybe he's not out there, Bones.
Maybe he's right here. Human heart."

Sharon Esther Lampert

The First Law of Nature is INSANITY

Measure the Pain!
Life is a Punishment

Measure the Pleasure
Life is a Gift

11 Esoteric Laws of Inextricability

ONLY GOD KNOWS **WHY?** AND GOD KNOWS BEST!

THE END OF FEEL GOOD PSYCHOBABBLE THAT NUMBS THE PAIN AND KEEP THEM SANE!

Is Life a Gift or a Punishment?

11 Absolute Truths

Final Note

The First Law of Nature Is Insanity

If it was all up to me, I would hang a gargantuan, red, and electronic blinking billboard that reads:

WELCOME TO PLANET EARTH
WARNING: INSANITY RULES
CONDEMED! UNINHABITABLE!

Matter of fact, my acute sensitivity, is a personal suffering at times; and at other times a strength, if directed into my literary pursuits:

I, Sharon Esther Lampert, the Philosopher Queen, certainly, do not write to influence the reader in any way, shape, or form.

I write merely to communicate my perspicacious insights, and to share them with the readers.

If I also succeed in educating readers, then so be it, an added perk, as I cannot educate socialized human beings beyond their innate intelligence.

If I also succeed in enlightening readers, then so be it, another added bonus, as I cannot enlighten socialized human beings who prefer to live in a state of abysmal ignorance, deafening denial, and sheer stupidity.

If I also succeed in advancing and expanding the frontiers of human knowledge, then so be it, another added benefit of vast humanitarian dimensions.

Find the **LIGHT** and Live in the **LIGHT**!

Sharon Esther Lampert
Philosopher Queen

The Birth of a Philosopher Queen: Sharon Esther Lampert

At the age of nine, Sharon's **MOMMY** proclaimed, "My daughter is a poet, philosopher, and teacher. She is the Princess and the Pea! THE QUEEN HAS ARRIVED!"

As her vast imagination recalls, on the day she was born, her rough, tough, and tumble Holocaust survivor father was dumbfounded by her tears. How would his first blood relative, born after the Holocaust, a new big blue-eyed bundle of brand new baby survive in the big-bad world? Moments after her arrival, he exclaimed, "She just came out of the womb, and she is already crying... I don't understand! Nothing has happened to her yet! WHY is she already crying? How is she going to survive? Oh Veys Mir!"

And later, she recalls telling him, "You of all people, a Holocaust survivor, the sole surviving member of your immediate family, already knew that this place called Planet Earth was a god-forsaken place of pain, suffering, and death: the violence is indigenous. WHY did you bring me here to the big-bad world. WHY ME?."

Bittersweetly, it was very odd, how two very "shtarker" parents gave birth to a bouncing babe of extraordinary sensitivity and flaming intensity. How is it possible? WHY THEM?

Bittersweetly, so what if on the website, www.creativegenius.org, flaming intensity equals a creative genius. Anyhow, his little known fact does little to alleviate the inevitable mental anguish and suffering that is a natural consequence of this gifted reality of immortal genius.

Bittersweetly, during her childhood, she remembers answering WHY? to everything ever told to her:

"Darkly, WHY do I have to kill other living beings, cook them, and eat them to live?

Darkly, WHY don't animals have to cook?

Darkly, WHY do I have to have a period for thirty-three years? Why every single month? I am clearly in over my head!

Darkly, WHY isn't there a way out of this bloody mess, a pill or an operation?

Darkly, WHY is it too hot, to cold, too windy, too rainy to play outside?

Darkly, WHY do I have to catch a cold?

Darkly, WHY do I feel like I am going to die from the flu?

Darkly, WHY do I already need eye glasses in the fourth grade?

Darkly, WHY do I have cavities?

Darkly, WHY do I need to wear metal braces for five years?

And I really don't want to wear cat-eyed glasses and metal braces and have wavy hair all at the same time!

Darkly, clear-plastic braces did not as yet exist.

Sweetly, wire rims, contact lenses, and hair dryers were in vogue.

Bittersweetly, she looked closely at her parents and wondered, "WHY do I know these people?"

Darkly, she looked at the snotty-nosed boys in her class, "WHY will I have to marry one of them?"

Darkly, in the fourth grade, her cat died and she cried for two whole years after the fact, and she still wants to know, "WHY did my cat have to die?"

Darkly, WHY were all of my relatives murdered in the Holocaust?
In the deepest depths of her soul, she thought,
"First they force you to be born without your consent, and then to add insult to injury, they give you the business: racism, sexism, religious persecution, ageism, etc.

Darkly, every five minutes you have to rise above a situation!

Darkly, WHY are you giving me the business?" was the quintessential WHY.
WHY ME? is the concluding afterthought.

Darkly, WHY is all of this necessary?

What was considered normal was too hard! **"NORMAL IS TOO HARD!"** She exclaimed. A **Philosopher Queen** was born.

Enough already of her childhood!

At age 16, Sharon Esther left this note in the Wailing Wall in Jerusalem Israel:

Dear God,
I am not asking for help.
I am asking to be of help.
I am at yor service.
Sharon Esther Lampert

"The worst thing that has ever happened to me is that I was born.
The best thing that has ever happened to me is that I was born Jewish."
Philosopher Queen Sharon Esther Lampert
Princess Kadimah, 8TH Prophetess of Israel
PHOTON, SUPERHERO OF EDUCATION, smartgrades.com

P.S. **Find the Light and Live in the Light!**

Sharon Esther Lampert

Ancient Philosophers

* Aenisedemus
* Alcmaeon of Croton
* Alexander of Aphrodisias
* Alexander Polyhistor, Lucius Cornelius
* Anaxagoras
* Anaximander
* Anaximenes
* Antisthenes
* Arcesilaus
* Archelaus of Athens
* Archytas of Tarentum
* Aristotle
* Aurelius, Marcus
* Carneades
* Chrysippus
* Cicero, Marcus Tullius
* Cleanthes
* Confucius
* Critias
* Democritus
* Diogenes Laertius
* Diogenes of Apollonia
* Diogenes of Sinope
* Diotima of Mantinea
* Empedocles
* Empiricus, Sextus
* Epictetus
* Epicurus
* Euclides
* Heraclitus
* Hippias
* Hippon of Samos
* Lao Tzu
* Leucippus
* Lucretius
* Melissus of Samos
* Mencius
* Menippus
* Philo of Alexandria
* Philolaus
* Plato
* Protagoras
* Pyrrho
* Pythagoras
* Socrates
* Speusippus
* Sung-Tzu
* Thales
* Theophrastus
* Xenocrates
* Xenophanes
* Xenophon
* Zeno of Citium
* Zeno of Elea

Medieval Philosophers

* Abelard, Peter
* Albert of Saxony
* Alyngton, Robert
* Anselm of Canterbury
* Aquinas, Thomas
* Augustine of Hippo
* Auriol, Peter
* Averroes
* Avicenna
* Bacon, Roger
* Boethius, Anicius Manlius Severinus
* Buridan, John
* Damian, Peter
* Dante Alighieri
* Duns Scotus, John
* Eckhart, Meister Johannes
* Erfurt, Thomas of
* Eriugena, John Scotus
* Farabi
* Francis of Marchia
* Gersonides
* Ghazali
* Giles of Rome
* Godfrey of Fontaines
* Gregory of Rimini
* Herbert of Cherbury, Edward
* Heytesbury, William
* Holcot, Robert
* Hypatia
* Kilvington, Richard
* Kindi
* Magnus, Albertus
* Maimonides, Moses

* Marsilius of Inghen
* Nicholas of Autrecourt
* Ockham, William of
* Paul of Venice
* Penbygull, William
* Peter of Spain
* Plotinus
* Porphyry
* Richard the Sophister
* Roscelin, Johann
* Rufus of Cornwall, Richard
* Saadya Gaon
* Salisbury, John of
* Sharpe, Johannes
* William of Auvergne
* William of Champeaux
* William of Conches
* William of Moerbeke
* Wyclif, John

Renaissance Philosophers

* Agrippa, Heinrich Cornelius
* Argyropoulos, John
* Bacon, Francis
* Barbaro, Ermolao
* Bessarion, John
* Bodin, Jean
* Boehme, Jacob
* Bruni, Leonardo
* Bruno, Giordano
* Bude, Guillaume
* Burgersdijk, Franco
* Cajetan, Tommaso de Vio
* Campanella, Tommaso
* Cano, Melchior
* Cesalpino, Andrea
* Charron, Pierre
* Chrysoloras, Manuel
* Desgabets, Robert
* Eck, Johann
* Erasmus, Desiderius
* Ficino, Marsilio
* Galilei, Galileo
* Guicciardini, Francesco
* Landino, Cristoforo
* Las Casas, Bartoleme de
* Lipsius, Justus
* Luther, Martin
* Machiavelli, Niccolo
* Montaigne, Michel de
* More, Thomas
* Muret, Marc-Antoine de

* Nicholas of Cusa
* Oresme, Nicolas
* Palmieri, Matteo
* Pico della Mirandola, Giovanni
* Pomponazzi, Pietro
* Ramus, Peter
* Scaliger, Julius Caesar
* Suarez, Francisco
* Vair, Guillaume du
* Valla, Lorenzo
* Vanini, Giulio Cesare
* Vico, Giambattista
* Vitoria, Francisco de
* Vives, Juan Luis
* Zabarella, Jacopo

Early Modern Philosophers

* Arnauld, Antoine
* Astell, Mary
* Bayle, Pierre
* Beccaria, Cesare
* Bentham, Jeremy
* Berkeley, George
* Bolingbroke, Henry St. John
* Boyle, Robert
* Burke, Edmund
* Butler, Joseph
* Clarke, Samuel
* Collins, Anthony
* Condillac, Ettiene Bonnot de
* Cruz, Sor Juana Ines de la
* Cudworth, Ralph
* Descartes, Rene
* Diderot, Denis
* Elizabeth of Bohemia
* Gassendi, Pierre
* Geulincx, Arnold
* Hartley, David
* Herder, Johann Gottfried von
* Hobbes, Thomas
* Holbach, Paul-Henri Thiry, Baron d'
* Hume, David
* Jefferson, Thomas
* Johnson, Samuel
* Kant, Immanuel
* LeGrand, Antoine
* Leibniz, Gottfried Wilhelm
* Locke, John
* Malebranche, Nicolas

* Masham, Damaris Cudworth
* Mendelssohn, Moses
* Mersenne, Marin
* Montesquieu, Charles-Louis de
  Secondat, Baron de
* Newton, Isaac
* Paine, Thomas
* Pascal, Blaise
* Reid, Thomas
* Rousseau, Jean-Jacques
* Shaftesbury, Earl of
* Sidney, Algernon
* Smith, Adam
* Spinoza, Baruch
* Voltaire
* Wasa, Kristina
* Wollstonecraft, Mary

19th Century Philosophers

* Alcott, Amos
* Austin, John
* Bakunin, Mikhael
* Bastiat, Frederic
* Bauer, Bruno
* Bolzano, Bernard
* Boole, George
* Bosanquet, Bernard
* Bradley, Francis Herbert
* Brentano, Franz
* Caird, Edward
* Cantor, Georg
* Comte, August
* Constant, Benjamin
* Dilthey, Wilhelm
* Donoso Cortes, Juan
* Emerson, Ralph Waldo
* Engels, Friedrich
* Eucken, Rudolph
* Federov, Nikolai Fedorovich
* Feuerbach, Ludwig
* Fichte, Immanuel
* Fichte, Johann Gottlieb
* Frege, Gottlob
* Green, Thomas Hill
* Hamilton, William
* Hegel, G.W.F.
* James, William
* Kierkegaard, Soren
* MacColl, Hugh
* Marx, Karl
* Meinong, Alexius

* Mill, Harriet Taylor
* Mill, John Stuart
* Natorp, Paul
* Nietzsche, Friedrich
* Peirce, Benjamin
* Peirce, Charles Sanders
* Rosmini, Antonio
* Schelling, Friedrich
* Schleiermacher, Friedrich
* Schopenhauer, Arthur
* Spencer, Herbert
* Thoreau, Henry David
* Whewell, William

20th Century Philosophers

* Abramowski, Edward
* Adler, Alfred
* Adorno, Theodor
* Ajdukiewicz, Kazimierz
* Althusser, Louis
* Ambrose, Alice
* Anscombe, G.E.M.
* Arendt, Hannah
* Austin, J.L.
* Ayer, A.J.
* Bakhtin, Mikhail
* Barth, Karl
* Barthes, Roland
* Bataille, George
* Baudrillard, Jean
* Beauvoir, Simone de
* Berdyaev, Nicholai
* Bergmann, Gustav
* Berlin, Isaiah
* Blondel, Maurice
* Bohr, Niels
* Bonhoeffer, Dietrich
* Brouwer, L.E.J.
* Brzozowski, Stanislaw
* Buber, Martin
* Camus, Albert
* Carnap, Rudolf
* Cassirer, Ernst
* Chesterton, G.K.
* Chomsky, Noam
* Church, Alonzo
* Churchland, Paul
* Chwistek, Leon

* Croce, Benedetto
* Czezowski, Tadeusz
* Davidson, Donald
* Dawkins, Richard
* Deleuze, Gilles
* Dennett, Daniel
* Derrida, Jacques
* Dewey, John
* DuBois, W.E.B.
* Dummett, Michael
* Einstein, Albert
* Fanon, Frantz
* Feyerabend, Paul
* Fleck, Ludwig
* Foucault, Michel
* Gadamer, Hans-Georg
* Gettier, Edmund
* Gilligan, Carol
* Godel, Kurt
* Goodman, Nelson
* Habermas, Jurgen
* Hartshorne, Charles
* Hayek, Friedrich
* Heidegger, Martin
* Hempel, Carl Gustav
* Husserl, Edmund
* Ingarden, Roman
* Jaspers, Karl
* Kelles-Krauz, Kazimierz
* Kojève, Alexandre
* Kotarbinski, Tadeusz
* Kripke, Saul
* Kristeva, Julia

Sharon Esther Lampert

20th Century Philosophers

* Krzywicki, Ludwik
* Kuhn, Thomas
* Langer, Suzanne
* Lesniewski, Stanislaw
* Levinas, Emmanuel
* Lewis, C.I.
* Lukasiewicz, Jan
* MacKinnon, Catharine
* Marcel, Gabriel
* Marcuse, Herbert
* Maritain, Jacques
* McTaggart, John
* Mead, George Herbert
* Merleau-Ponty, Maurice
* Moore, G.E.
* Natorp, Paul
* Nock, Albert Jay
* Nozick, Robert
* Oakeshott, Michael
* Ortega y Gasset, Jose
* Plantinga, Alvin
* Polanyi, Michael
* Popper, Karl
* Prior, Arthur
* Putnam, Hilary
* Quine, W.V.O.
* Rand, Ayn
* Rawls, John
* Reichenbach, Hans
* Ricoeur, Paul
* Rorty, Richard
* Russell, Bertrand
* Ryle, Gilbert

* Said, Edward
* Santayana, George
* Sartre, Jean-Paul
* Schlick, Moritz
* Schumpeter, Joseph
* Schutz, Alfred
* Searle, John
* Sellars, Wilfrid
* Shestov, Lev
* Strawson, Peter
* Tarski, Alfred
* Tatarkiewicz, Wladyslaw
* Tillich, Paul
* Turing, Alan
* Twardowski, Kazimierz
* Unamuno y Jugo, Miguel de
* Weber, Max
* Weil, Simone
* Whitehead, Alfred North
* Witkiewicz, Stanislaw
* Wittgenstein, Ludwig
* Znaniecki, Florian

GOD OF WHAT? Is Life a Gift or a Punishment?

Philosopher Queen Sharon Esther Lampert

Revelations: My Books Write Themselves!

1. **Unleash the Creator the God Within**
   10 Esoteric Laws of Genius and Creativity

2. **GOD TALKS TO ME - Who Knew God Was Such a Chatterbox?**
   A Working Definition of God — GOD IS GO! DO!
   Why is it **NORMAL** for 8-billion people to talk to God, but **CRAZY** if God talks to me?

3. **God of What?**
   11 Esoteric Laws of Inextricability - 11 Absolute Truths
   Is Life a Gift or a Punishment? Measure the Pain! Measure the Pleasure!

4. **THE 22 COMMANDMENTS**
   All You Will Ever Need to Know About God
   A Universal Moral Compass for All People, For All Religions, and For All Time

5. Women Have All the Power But Have Never Learned How to Use It

6. The Sperm Manifesto: 10 Rules for the Road

7. 10 MIRACLES: What Happens When You Free Your Mind of NEGATIVITY?

The Conceptualization of BIG IDEAS Using One Letter of the Alphabet

8. Temporary Insanity: We Are Building Our Lives on a **S**and Trap
   — Written in Letter S

9. **C**UPID: Language of Love
   — Written in Letter C

10. DESTINY: **D**ARE TO **D**REAM Are You Living Life By **D**EFAULT or By **D**ESIGN?
    — Written in Letter D

Sharon Esther Lampert

NYU

Honored Sharon Lampert
with an Award for
"Multi-Interdisciplinary Studies"
YOUTUBE video

Poet
Philosopher
Peacemaker
Prophet
Princess & Pea
PINUP
Performer:Vocalist
Player: Jock
Paladin of Education
PHOTON SUPERHERO
Princess Kadimah
President
Publisher
Producer
Psychobiologist—Rockefeller U.
Piano-Playing Cat
Playdate
Phoenix
Prodigy

Websites:
SharonEstherLampert.com
PhilosopherQueen.com
WorldFamousPoems.com
VeryExtraSpecial.com
PoetryEssentialService.com
PoetryJewels.com
Schmaltzy.com
GodofWhat.com
TrueLoveBurnsEternal.com
LoveYouMoreThanYesterday.com
WinAtThin.com
SillyLittleBoys.com
PlannerParExcellence.com
FloridaRetirementPlanner.com
WritersRunTheWorld.com
PalmBeachBookPublisher.com

Education
Smartgrades.com
BooksNotBombs.com
EverydayanEasyA.com

Gift Shop:
HappyGrandparenting.com
GodIsGoDo.com
WorldPeaceEquation.com
ArtHeart.store
BooksArePowerful.com

THE 22 COMMANDMENTS
All You Will Ever Need to Know About God

A Universal Moral Compass for All People
For All People, For All Religions, For All Time

1. **LIFE** Over Death

2. **STRENGTH** Over Weakness

3. **DEED** Over Sin

4. **LOVE** Over Hatred

5. **TRUTH** Over Lie

6. **COURAGE** Over Fear

7. **OPTIMISM** Over Pessimism

8. **SHARING** Over Selfishness

9. **PRAISE** Over Criticism

10. **LOYALTY** Over Abandonment

11. **RESPONSIBILITY** Over Blame

12. **GRATITUDE** Over Grievances

13. **REWARD** Over Punishment

14. **ALLIES** Over Enemies

15. **CREATION** Over Destruction

16. **EDUCATION** Over Ignorance

17. **COOPERATION** Over Competition

18. **FREEDOM** Over Oppression

19. **COMPASSION** Over Indifference

20. **FORGIVENESS** Over Revenge

21. **PEACE** Over War

22. **JOY** Over Suffering

By Sharon Esther Lampert
Princess Kadimah, 8TH Prophetess of Israel
Read My Book: "**THE 22 COMMANDMENTS**"
Founder of KADIMAISM

About the Prodigy
Gifted: Born with an Extra Body Part: "Creative Apparatus"

Prodigy — Princess & Pea!
Unleash The Creator The God Within: 10 Esoteric Laws of Genius and Creativity

Poet — One of The World's Greatest Poets — 22 + Poetry Books
Poetry World Record: 120 Words of Rhyme
The Greatest Poems Ever Written on Extraordinary World Events
http://Famouspoetsandpoems.com/Poets.html

Prophet
- God Talks to Me: A Working Definition of God — GOD IS GO! DO!
- 22 Commandments: All You Will Ever Need to Know About God

Philosopher Queen
- Temporary Insanity: We Are Building Our Lives on a Sand Trap — Written In Letter S
- God of What? 10 Esoteric Laws of Inextricability
- Sperm Manifesto: 10 Rules for the Road
- Women Have All the Power But Have Never Learned How to Use It

Peacemaker
World Peace Equation.com

Paladin of Education — PHOTON SUPERHERO OF EDUCATION — 25 Books+
SMARTGRADES BRAIN POWER REVOLUTION
- The Silent Crisis Destroying Americas Brightest Minds - BOOK OF THE MONTH
- Everyday An Easy A!

Pioneer
- Silly Little Boys: 40 Rules of Manhood — For Men of All Ages!
- CUPID: Language of Love — Written In Letter C
- DESTINY: Are You Living Life by Default or by Design? — Written In Letter D
- PUBLISH: The Secret Sauce of Book Sales — Written In Letter P
- 10 Miracles: What Happens When You Free Your Mind of Negativity?
- Love You More Than Yesterday: 14 Relationship Strategies for Happily After Ever
- WIN AT THIN: FAT ME SKINNY ME — What Works! What Doesn't

Princess Kadimah
8TH PROPHETESS OF ISRAEL: THE 22 COMMANDMENTS

PINUP
SEXIEST CREATIVE GENIUS IN HUMAN HISTORY

Artists March to the Beat of a Different Drummer
Sharon Esther Lampert Marches to the Beat of an Entire Orchestra

Poet, Philosopher, Prophet, Peacemaker
Paladin of Education, Princess & Pea
Phoenix, PHOTON, PINUP, Prodigy

Blue-Eyed. Brilliant. Beautiful. Buxom. Books

Sharon Esther Lampert was born an **OLD SOUL** — She was never young! Sharon is a lefty.
At age nine, her mother declared: "My daughter is a poet, philosopher, and teacher!" She nicknamed her daughter, "The Princess and Pea!" "THE QUEEN HAS ARRIVED!"

Sharon's greatest literary works woke her up in the middle of the night — and made her get up out of bed — and write them down. Sharon writes an entire book in one day!

Sharon's mother was the sole person in Sharon's life who knew who she was from the **INSIDE OUT**! Her beloved mother also knew to her very last breath... the exact day and to the minute when she would die! (Eve Paikoff Lampert: June 3, 1925 — May 5, 1985).

Later in life, Sharon purchases a green-pea pendant, at the Broadway show, "Once Upon a Mattress" starring Sarah Jessica Parker. She wore the green pea every day around her neck with a beautiful Jewish-star pendant from Haifa, Israel.

Sharon Esther's Gifts Are Metaphysical — Beyond the Scope of Scientific Inquiry

There Are No Rough Drafts! — Revelation: The Books Write Themselves!

Sharon Has 4 Books with GOD in the Title

"A LIST" Sharon Esther Lampert is One of the World's Greatest Poets
http://famouspoetsandpoems.com/poets.html

#1 Poetry Website for Student Poetry Projects
On a global scale, Sharon's poetry is used by teachers for their poetry lesson plans, and by students for their poetry school projects (see student FAN MAIL).

New York University Awards — YOUTUBE Videos
Sharon Esther earned three degrees from NYU — and she was honored with two NYU awards. Sharon represented her class at her graduation — and was honored with an award for "Multi-Interdisciplinary Studies." She also played on the NYU Women's Varsity Basketball team as a center in the $16-million Coles Sports Center. Sharon won an "NYU Weightlifting Contest"— Sharon was the sole contestant — so she won! (Washington Square News article).

Sharon Esther Lampert

PINUP

SEXIEST CREATIVE GENIUS IN HUMAN HISTORY

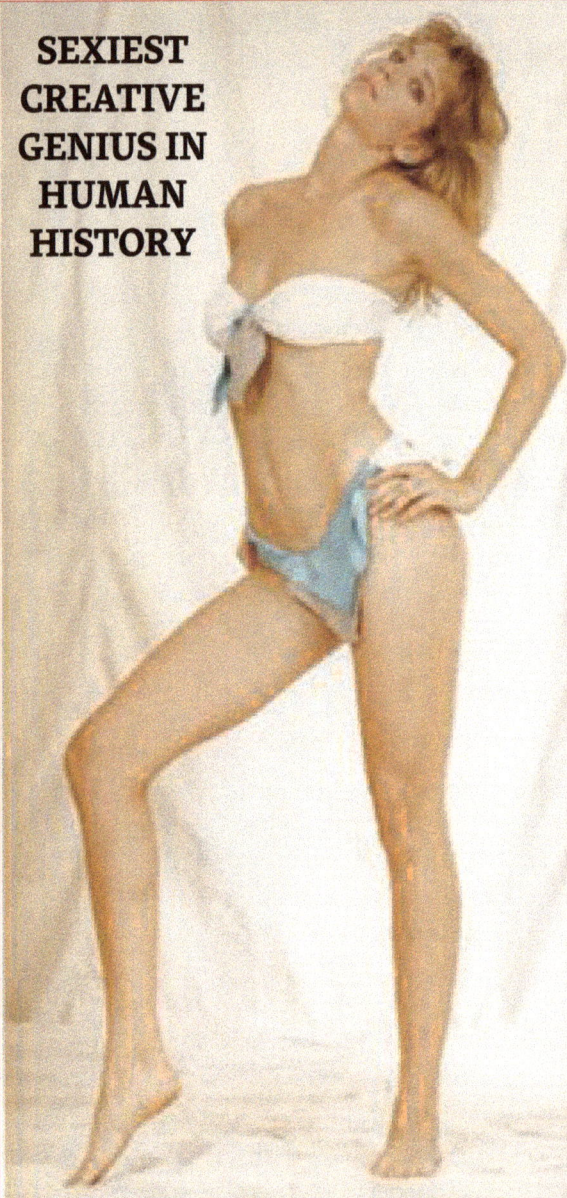

MYLIFE Is an OPENBOOK, to KNOWME Is to README

FAN MAIL
FANS@SharonEstherLampert.com

A PHENOMENON...
SHARON ESTHER LAMPERT

Lithe and lovely ... like a fawn.
This lady fascinates me ... from dusk till dawn.
Feminine and comely ... she's beyond belief
A blue-beam from her eyes ... is my soothing relief.

Girlish in her braces ... maidenly in her style
I yearn for her embraces ... and adore her friendly smile.
As tasteful as any artist ... you'll ever see
She's a compendium of class ... from A to Z.

If you'd like to see a figure, that puts Venus to shame
Behold her in a swimsuit, and your passions will aflame.
Ever exuding goodness . . . guided from above
Miss Sharon is the essence, and epitome of Love.

She's the inspiration of sages, and also fools like me
And the most magnificent female, I'm sure I'll ever see.
The nights are now endearing, & never filled with doubt
I sometimes wake up singing, cause it's Sharon . . .
I dream about.

Affectionately, . .
A devoted fan,
—Harry McVeety

FAN MAIL

FANS@SharonEstherLampert.com

Dear Sharon,

You are not only an exquisite poet, you're beautiful! Am smitten by your luminous beingness. Are you an angel in disguise--a so-called malachim in Hebrew if I am not mistaken.

Thank you for your wondeful open-hearted response. Your photo will sit next to those of Gautama Buddha and the Blessed Virgin Mary.

I will follow your sound esoteric advise regarding the positioning of your photo and the two other icons. I am deeply impressed that you are very conscious about the concept of sacred space and the flow of spiritual energy. So please send me your precious photo as soon as possible.

P.S. Will you be generous enough to send me your signed photo which I will place on the secret altar of my heart, lit by the menorah, the seven-stemmed candelabra of your inspiration, O mystical muse, O Rose of Sharon...

Your ardent fan and admirer,
— Felix Fojas, the cybercat with a mystical meow
Chico, CA, 95926

SOLVE ONE PROBLEM: EDUCATION: SAVE ENTIRE WORLD

Sharon Esther Lampert

My book was chosen as
BOOK OF THE MONTH
by the Alma Public
Library in Wisconsin,
**"The Silent Crisis
Destroying America's
Brightest Minds."**
ISBN: 978-1885872548

My Pen Name:
Sharon Rose Sugar

**SMARTGRADES BRAIN
POWER REVOLUTION**
Smartgrades.com
EverydayanEasyA.com
BooksNotBombs.com
PhotonSuperHero.com

- The 15 Stepping Stones of Academic Success
- The 15 Stumbling Blocks of Academic Failure
- 10 Learning Tools for Academic Excellence
- 40 Universal Gold Standards of Education
- Parenting for Academic Success

PALADIN OF EDUCATION & PHOTON SUPERHERO

KADIMAH PRESS: Gifts of Genius

Relevations: My Books Write Themselves!

Poet: The Greatest Poems Ever Written on Extraordinary World Events
Title: I Stole All the Words from the Dictionary
ISBN Hardcover: 978-1-885872-06-7
ISBN Paperback: 978-1-885872-07-4
ISBN E-Book: 978-1-885872-08-1

22+ BOOKS OF POETRY

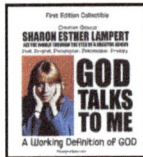

Prophet: WORLD PREMIERE!
Title: GOD TALKS TO ME: A WORKING DEFINITION OF GOD GOD IS GO! DO!
WHO KNEW GOD WAS SUCH A CHATTERBOX?
ISBN Hardcover: 978-1-885872-33-3
ISBN Paperback: 978-1-885872-34-0
ISBN E-Book: 978-1-885872-36-4

25+ BOOKS EDUCATION

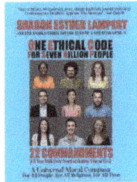

Prophet: WORLD PREMIERE!
Title: The 22 Commandments: All You Will Ever Need to Know About God
A Universal Moral Compass For All People, For All Religions, For All Time
ISBN Hardcover: 978-1-885872-03-6
ISBN Paperback: 978-1-885872-04-3
ISBN E-Book: 978-1-885872-05-0

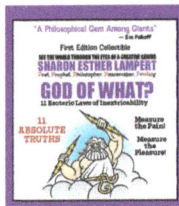

Philosopher: WORLD PREMIERE!
Title: God of What? 11 Esoteric Laws of Inextricability - 11 Absolute Truths
Is Life a Gift or a Punishment? Measure the Pain! Measure the Pleasure!
ISBN Hardcover: 978-1-885872-00-5
ISBN Paperback: 978-1-885872-01-2
ISBN E-Book: 978-1-885872-02-9
GodofWhat.com

Prodigy: WORLD PREMIERE!
Title: Unleash the Creator The God Within: 10 Esoteric Laws of Genius and Creativity
ISBN Hardcover: 978-1-885872-21-0
ISBN Paperback: 978-1-885872-22-7
ISBN E-Book: 978-1-885872-23-4

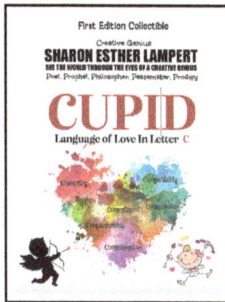

Prodigy: WORLD PREMIERE!
Title: CUPID: Language of Love — Written in Letter C
ISBN Hardcover: 978-1-885872-55-5
ISBN Paperback: 978-1-885872-56-2
ISBN E-Book: 978-1-885872-57-9
SharonEstherLampert.com

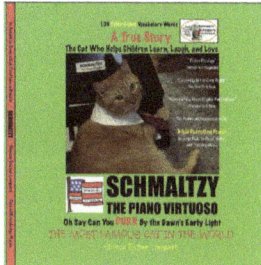

Popular: Children's Book, Ages 8-12
Title: SCHMALTZY: IN AMERICA, EVEN A CAT CAN HAVE A DREAM
ISBN Hardcover: 978-1-885872-39-5
ISBN Paperback: 978-1-885872-38-8
ISBN E-Book: 978-1-885872-37-1
Schmaltzy.com

COLOR-CODED
VOCABULARY WORDS

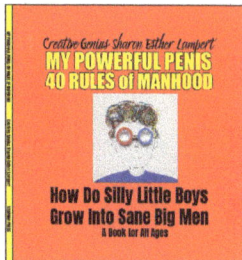

Popular: WORLD PREMIERE
Title: SILLY LITTLE BOYS: 40 RULES OF MANHOOD
HOW DO SILLY LITTLE BOYS GROW INTO SANE BIG MEN
14 Global Catastrophes of Violence Against Women
ISBN Hardcover: 978-1-885872-29-6
ISBN Paperback: 978-1-885872-35-7
ISBN E-Book: 978-1-885872-41-8
SillyLittleBoys.com

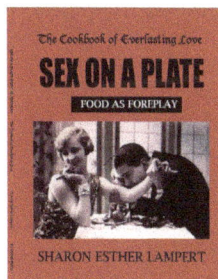

Popular: Every Great Relationship Begins with the Perfect Meal
Title: SEX ON A PLATE: FOOD AS FOREPLAY
THE COOKBOOK OF EVERLASTING LOVE
ISBN Hardcover: 978-1-885872-46-3
ISBN Paperback: 978-1-885872-48-7
ISBN E-Book: 978-1-885872-47-0
TrueLoveBurnsEternal.com

THANK YOU

Count Your Blessings. Practice Gratitude.

Blessing 1. My Genetics, Two Sets of Artsy-Fartsy Genes and Gift of Genius — Lefty! —Like **MOMMY**!
- Genetic Inheritance: Painter Maternal Grandfather Benjamin Paikoff &
  Sculptor Father Abraham Lampert (Exhibit in Museum of Jewish Heritage, NYC)
- Vocalist: Ashira Orchestra, 18 Years: Ramaz Women's Service (YOUTUBE video)
- Athlete: "Faster Than Any Boy, Anytime, Anywhere, Any Age!"

Blessing 2. My Life: Dawn of Digital Revolution
- APPLE: The Golden Age of Personal Computers
- ADOBE: The Golden Age of Creativity
- INGRAM: The Golden Age of Publishing
- SOCIAL MEDIA: The Golden Age of Internet & Global Communication
- iTUNES: The Golden Age of Music and Lyrics

Blessing 3. My Loved Ones
- Selflove: "Mindfulness, Meditation, Mantra, and Music Mitigates Madness!"
- Unconditional True Love: My **MOMMY** Eve Paikoff Lampert
- My PURRfect Children: SCHMALTZY and FALAFEL, Schmaltzy.com
- My "Friends First and Forever, and Family" NYU Tisch Professor Karl Bardosh
- My **Meta**physical Sister: Poet on a Mission Hannah Sezenes, "ELI, ELI"
- My 7 Practice Husbands, Artist—Muses, Dates, and NYC Night Life
- My Bubbe Esther Tulkoff, EstherTulkoff.com

Blessing 4. My NYU Education, Educators, and Awards
My NYU Education: BA, MA, MA and AWARDS, YOUTUBE video
- NYU Professor Laurin Raiken
  NYU "Multi-Interdisciplinary Award" and MA Class Representative at Graduation
- Rockefeller University, NYC, Publication: "Hyperphagia and Obesity Induced by
  Neuropeptide Y" — Lab of Dr. Sarah Leibowitz and Dr. Glen Stanley
- AWARD: 100-Year Scholarship Award Winner, Presented by NYC Mayor Edward Koch
- AWARD: Empire Science Scholarship Award Winner
- AWARD: Jerusalem Fellowship Award, Aish Hatorah, Israel
- AWARD: First Prize: Upper East Side Resident Writing Contest
- Voice Teachers: Andy Anselmo of The Singer's Forum, NYC & Estelle Leibling
- Cantor Sherwin Goffin of LSS & Riva Alper of RAMAZ Women's Service (18 Years)

Blessing 5. My Sports
- NYC Marathon
- Basketball: NYU Women's Varsity Basketball Team, Center, NYU Coach Sherri Pickard
- NYU Weightlifting Contest Winner! $16 Million Coles Sports Center (solo contestant — so I won!)
- Basketball: NYC Urban Professional League
- B-Ball Coaches Chicago Bulls Phil Jackson and Boston Celtics Bill Walton, Omega Institute, NY
- Basketball and Softball — Coach Sandy Pyonin
- Skiing: Heavenly, Lake Tahoe, Nevada
- Tennis: NYC Central Park Tennis Courts
- Baseball, Hall of Fame: Coaches Wilma Briggs and Jean Harding, Omega Institute, NY

Blessing 6. My Inspirations
- ISRAEL: "AM YISRAEL CHAI!" Lambs to Slaughter to Lions & Light of the World: 22% of Nobel Prizes!
- NYC: The Golden Age of Personal Freedom & Creative Self-Expression
- AMERICA: Land of Unlimited Possibility, Potential, and Prosperity!

NYU Gallatin Professor
Laurin Raiken and Me at
My Graduation

NYU Tisch Professor
Karl Bardosh and Me
Friend & Family Forever!

LITERATURE IS POWERFUL BEYOND WORDS FOR IT CREATES WORLDS

— Sharon Esther Lampert

EVERY THOUGHT IN YOUR HEAD WAS PUT THERE BY A WRITER

— Sharon Esther Lampert

Please Keep in Touch!
Website, Facebook, Twitter, Instagram, YOUTUBE, Pinterest
FANS@SharonEstherLampert.com

Revelations: My Books Write Themselves!
I Am Mortal. My Books Are Immortal.
Please Handle My Books Gently.
My Books Are My Remains.

This book was compiled in four parts:
Part 1. **Birth of Idea** — 1999
Part 2. Format Book — 2009
Part 3. 10 Essays — 2009
Part 4. Publish — December 2022

Sharon Esther Lampert
SEE THE WORLD THROUGH THE EYES OF A CREATIVE GENIUS

Poet, Philosopher, Prophet, Peacemaker, Paladin of Education, Princess, Prodigy

FANS@SharonEstherLampert.com

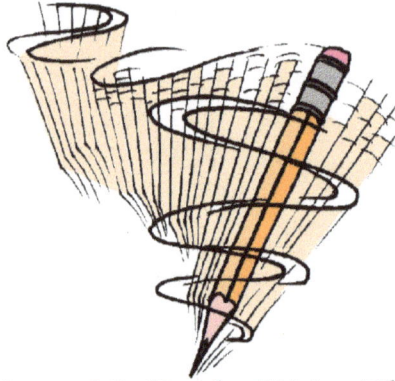

EDUCATION FAIR USE NOTICE
This book contains material which may not have been authorized by the copyright owners. We are making such material available in our efforts to advance understanding of social justice, political, human rights and democracy issues. We believe this constitutes a 'fair use' of any such copyrighted material as provided for in section 107 of the US Copyright Law.

www.ingramcontent.com/pod-product-compliance
Lightning Source LLC
Chambersburg PA
CBHW052338210326
41597CB00031B/5302